Ponderings of a Poet

AF624571

Sandeep Deol

BookLeaf Publishing
India | USA | UK

Ponderings of a Poet © 2023 Sandeep Deol

All rights reserved.

No part of this publication may be reproduced, stored in a retrieval system, or transmitted, in any form or by any means, electronic, mechanical, photocopying, recording, or otherwise, without the prior written permission of the presenters.

Sandeep Deol asserts the moral right to be identified as the author of this work.

Presentation by *BookLeaf Publishing*

Web: www.bookleafpub.com

E-mail: info@bookleafpub.com

ISBN: 9789357442459

First edition 2023

I dedicate this to my husband. Without his encouragement, I probably would not have signed up for this poetry challenge and I ended up really enjoying it. I couldn't have asked for a better life partner.

ACKNOWLEDGEMENT

Thank you to BookLeaf Publishing for advertising this poetry challenge. It really helped me practice shorter forms of daily writing whilst also finding creative ways to express some important thoughts.

PREFACE

One day whilst scrolling the internet, a poetry challenge was noticed on social media. Months later, this booklet of poetry was made. The poetry competition involved writing a poem a day for 21 days (extensions were allowed which was great because daily inspiration was not always there). As an aspiring writer, this was great practice and really awoke a need to evaluate some important life thoughts.

If only...

If only I were less brazen,
Then perhaps I could blend in better.

If only I were 10 pounds thinner,
So I wouldn't dread going out.

If only I were a little smarter,
Because then I wouldn't be talked down to.

If only I were a little older,
That way I wouldn't always be seen as the baby.

But most importantly, most importantly of all…

If only I could accept myself more consistently.

If only I could remember…
for every single moment,
of every single day,
That I am in fact okay.

Resolving Conflict

During that winter…
She faced the confrontation,
And she was now free.

Heart

You can try to intimidate me
With your fancy words and quick wit
But I will break each word down.

You can attempt to manipulate me
And make me feel insecure
But I have too much self-love.

You can take advantage of my kindness
By trying to emotionally guilt me
But that too has its limits.

You may find it worthwhile to compete with me
To validate yourself and feel better
But I only choose to compete with myself.

You may think I'm not as connected as you
That I can’t fix a problem by using my contacts
But I can network my way around when needed.

Because the one thing you can never do;
The thing that many have tried to do,
Is break my spirit, for it is true;
I have too much heart not to see things through.

Time

As she lay there, running out of breath,
Listening to the machines around her,
Feeling odd in that clinical atmosphere,
She began to think back...

She thought back to the places she'd never been,
She reminisced about the food she never tried,
The time she refused to spend on her passion,
Choosing to instead sit safely behind a desk.
She thought of the children she never had;
She was never quite ready…
Looking now to the moments left ahead of her,
She wished for more time,
When in the past she never quite had the time,
And just like that she closed her eyes for the
very last time.

Fighter

Round one.
He takes a punch to the right;
He takes another to the left;
And he thinks about the title slipping away.

Round two.
He now questions his previous opponents,
And whether they were truly worthy,
Or whether he's had an easy ride staying on top.

Round three.
He fears he'll lose it all now…
The money, the cars, the house…
And stop being able to provide for his family.

Round four.
He fears his legacy will crumble,
And that after all the blood, sweat and tears…
He will be remembered as a loser, a coward.

Before round five she appears in his corner.
He turns to her and says "I can't do this."
To which she replies with the following:

"I have seen you fight until the last bell rings.

I’ve seen you take more beatings than any other.
Yet still, you get back up and fight.
And you fight with heart, with soul.
If you think you can’t do this, we forfeit,
But I don’t think that’s why you’re saying this.
I think you feel guilty over losing the last fight;
Because you feel you let your coach down.
I think you feel scared that you might lose;
Because now you have possessions to lose.
You feel disillusioned from winning before;
Winning fights that turned out to be fixed.
But I also know that if you don’t finish this…
You will continue to feel all these things,
And when you’re fighting days are over,
And when it’s just you and me left,
You won’t be able to live with yourself;
Because you are a fighter through and through,
And since I have known you, you’ve never quit.
So you need to go out there and resolve this;
Because no matter what the size of that guy is,
Your heart is ten times bigger.”

“And if I lose?” He asks.
“Then you lose.” She replies.
“But you lose with nothing to hide behind,
You lose after giving it everything you’ve got,
And I know you can live with that.
You got here by losing as much as winning!
Win or lose, you’ve already won in life,

You've already proved you're a champion."
He gets up...

Round 5 to 11 merge into one endless fight,
But his opponent becomes fatigued.
By round 12, he knocks his opponent out.
As he stands there whilst the crowd cheers,
He doesn't think of the title.
He doesn't recall the material possessions.
He doesn't care about what everyone else thinks.
He simply looks for the woman.
Because she's been there from the beginning,
Fuelling his drive for success with love.
Without her, he would be no champion.
As she stands there staring at him, she thinks...
Without him she wouldn't be such a believer..
He is a fighter in that ring,
Just as she is a fighter for their relationship,
And that's why this is ultimately a love story.

Forgive Me.

Once there was an elderly man,
Who would pray every single day.
He would say "pray whenever you can"
When trying to show others the right way.

One day he went to the store to buy some salt.
The owner gave him too much change.
The elderly man took it and decided to bolt,
Only afterwards he started to feel strange…

Once home, he went straight to the prayer room,
And said forgive me Father for I have sinned.
After this he was no longer filled with gloom,
But instead, he smiled and grinned.

The next day he ran into a friend who had
recently split from his wife.
Instead of politely refraining from bringing it up,
He bluntly addressed it, as though stabbing his
friend with a verbal knife.
Only later, he began to feel remorse as he sipped
from his cup…

That's why he went straight to the prayer room,
And said forgive me Father for I have sinned.

After this he was no longer filled with gloom,
But instead, he smiled and grinned.

A week later, the elderly man went to a homeless shelter.
He laid out all his donations in a box on the floor,
But as he did, he noticed a shiny, new, projector,
So he slyly grabbed it as he walked through the door.

Guiltily, he went straight to the prayer room,
And said forgive me Father for I have sinned.
After this he was no longer filled with gloom,
But instead, he simply smiled and grinned.

Later, he went for a nap after his daily meditation,
Only this time he did not wake up to his normal life,
But as an ant, with simply no explanation.
Realising how small he was, he became incredibly strife.

He asked why this happened after all the time he had dedicated to praying.
He was convinced he had done everything in his power to live well,

And as he questioned this, he could hear a voice from above saying;
“Because without the appropriate action, prayer is simply a shell.”

Settling

I was not meant to sit behind a desk,
And follow orders until the day I die.
My parents worked their fingers to the bone,
So that I could have the opportunity to rise.

I will not waste away my life by playing it safe.
For I have only one life to play.
My parents worked their fingers to the bone,
Because there are better things for me to face.

I will not wait for another white hair or wrinkle.
Waiting is my greatest growing fear,
My parents worked their fingers to the bone,
So that one day I could shine and twinkle.

I do not deem failure a filthy word.
Because from failure I seek strength.
My parents worked their fingers to the bone,
So that I could keep trying, undeterred.

I thought I had it all; typing and clicking my life away.
Faces were impressed by my money, my success.

As I’m talked down to by those who cannot lead.
Thrown under the bus, by those consumed with greed.
Derived of spare time during their 3 hour lunches,
But faces were impressed by my money, my success.

Until I finally had the courage to see…

I was not meant to sit behind a desk,
And follow orders until the day I die.
My parents worked their fingers to the bone,
So that I could have the opportunity to rise.

15 Minutes of Fame

Whether it's entering a villa to find love to tame,
Or finding someone to publicly blame,
Everyone's after it; those 15 minutes of fame.
Chasing it with absolutely no shame.

Even committing a heinous crime…
Seems to motivate people to find their time-
In front of the cameras so they can shine;
To perhaps tell their story; make a 'dime'.

We were all forewarned in stories and words…
He watches us all; we're all being observed.
Yet despite warnings that left us feeling
disturbed,
All forms of reality TV later emerged.

The venom that's spit; it fuels us.
Everyone decides to make a big fuss.
Not over current affairs that should be discussed,
But whether that 'fella on real housewives
looked sus.'

Gathering together and growing the hate,
As our compassion begins to slowly deflate,
Dehumanising real people and their fate,

Simply so we can have fun and socially berate.

I could go on and on, but the time has come;
To watch the latest Kardashians with Mum,
For even though we've reached new levels of
dumb…
I can't help but watch, be amazed by the
glamour and succumb.

The hometown blues

Slumming it here is what they think I did;
Loveless, this place is seen as an endless pit.
Over the park you can see Windsor Castle,
Ugliness everywhere else; nothing but hassle.
Growing up whilst told this place has no hope.
Hoping that perhaps this place isn't a joke.

Without doubt, the people make the town.
And I recall this as I walk past the frowns.
Sadly, yes, due to the council it's not the same…

Nevertheless I was schooled well for free.
Old friends made and kept through the debris;
Then of course; family memories full of glee.

So, before people talk trash about this place.
Humbly reminisce over this old, glorious space.
In the old days, there was plenty to embrace;
Though not everyone can utilise and create
!

The label that almost held me back.

'This is the one that's left'
That's how I'm now identified.
No name, no description, no background.
I am simply the one that's left.

I have defied my academic limitations.
I have exceeded my work ethic expectations.
I maintain a respectable appearance.
Yet I am still marked as 'the one that's left'.

As I near my thirties, the mark gets stronger…
My successes until now grow fainter…
Slowly fading away…
As the failure of ending my singleton ways…
Looms closer.

I no longer recall the defining experiences,
But simply my dating failures.
Failures on my end.
Failures on theirs…

'There must be something wrong with her.'
'She probably already has a secret boyfriend'

Then there are the comments made to my face;
"My dear it's only harder when you're older!"
But that would mean being marked forever…
Like a carton of milk on the shelf, unbudged-
Which expires, grows mouldy and sours.

As more marry before me at a younger age,
I am again met with perplexed faces;
Questioning why I cannot find a man,
After how hard I've worked to become a 'catch'.

Then the most remarkable thing happened…
I stopped caring.

I regained my memories of self-identity.
I enjoyed my new feeling of independence.
I became grateful for the things I do have,
And stopped focussing on what I don't have.

Then this newfound energy from within…
Began to shine like sunshine and rainbows,
And attracted potential partners;
Until I met my partner for life.

Now I'm no longer the one that's left,
Because I recalled what it means to be me,
Because I found gratitude in all that I have,
Because I refused to be defined by a label,
Finally, I am no longer 'the one that is left'.

Ego

Batting those pretty, blue eyes,
To get that girl; your prize.
Showing off that fair coloured skin,
To keep it a mystery; where you've been.

Gushing your way through life;
Accompanied by sweet, little lies,
Along with that hunger, that drive.
With ease, you try and you thrive.

But this time something's different…
What once started as a magnetic current;
Has halted; the girl has become resistant,
You try harder, she becomes belligerent.

For what is this feeling for the blue-eyed boy…
To be the one who feels used like a toy?
Is this how it feels on the other end of a ploy?
So, this is life when it's not an easy joy…

Let this boy's lesson be a lesson for you.
When you're pretty; life's easy to skate through,
But when tables turn and your karmic journey is due…
You learn the value of hard work; to actively pursue.

Home Team

One Winter I found,
There was no one else to love,
But you, my soulmate.

Clearly, I survived before you…
But knowing you know, why would I want to?

Daring me to be the best version of myself.
Endlessly supporting me.
Overexpanding my thoughts; challenging me.
Loving me whole, bleakness included.

Rhyming couplets, acrostic, or Haiku,
I can use them all and more to write about you.

They say it happens when it happens,
That's how I feel about you.
Always inevitable, written in our destiny.

My mentor, my love, my partner.
Together we could rule the world…

So come what may,
Let life challenge us some more.
For together there is nothing we cannot conquer.
Despite all that we've faced, we soar.

The human condition

Never was a bond so strong,
than that shared during grief.
Humanising us as we feel wronged.
Humbling us whilst we feel disbelief.

Though I'm grateful for all I've been given,
I can't understand why even the purest hearts,
Could fade away so painfully, so unforgivingly.

But never was a bond so strong,
than that shared during grief.
Humanising us as we feel wronged.
Humbling us whilst we feel disbelief.

It is often believed that life is a test,
Or that we are given only what we can handle.
Or that life is karmic, hence we try to be our best
But the amount of uncertainty is ample.

But I am certain that never was a bond so strong,
than that shared during grief.
Humanising us as we feel wronged.
Humbling us whilst we feel disbelief.

Isn't it incredible how powerful one can feel?

Or amazing how confidence can transform you?
But still, from mortality you cannot heal.
But still, to steer from death, one cannot do.

And so, take comfort in this if nothing else…

Never was a bond so strong,
than that shared during grief.
Humanising us as we feel wronged.
Humbling us whilst we feel disbelief.

To our loved souls that rest in peace…
We admired your fight until the end…
Although your life on earth has ceased,
In our hearts your life extends…

Never taken for granted…

An anthem for the working class.

First you grow up working class;
Mum and Dad work off their ass.
You get all the way through school,
So your CV has all the right jewels.

But then here's the kicker;
No experience, the employer sniggers…
Unlike those more privileged fools,
Who didn't study, but used the right 'tools'.

But you carry on working and finally get a job.
You work hard and save; no time to be a slob.
But then the housing prices increase,
Hopes of buying a new home decrease.

But wait; here comes the help to buy.
This is your time to purchase; to try.
But you get married to a really great guy,
And now you need a bigger space to buy.

Luckily the housing market crashes,
The amount to pay back slashes;
Only you transitioned into a whole new career,
From scratch, but you enjoy it, you'll persevere.

But then the mortgage rates have increased,
And the amount you can borrow has decreased,
But now the mortgage rates have gone down,
But now you can borrow less, so you frown.

January time already? Tax is due on the flat.
HMRC makes you pay upfront like a rat.
So the second income you've made,
Barely covers mortgage and tax; such a shame.

ISA to get a new £100k lifetime cap???
It helps those who haven't saved a 'scrap'???
Who are we kidding; it's to help the rich chaps;
To keep their overloaded wallets nice and FAT.

And so the cycle goes on and on and on…

The Government helps the rich get richer,
And the poor stay poorer.
Even when we save, invest and track our money,
We're deprived of our hard earned honey.

But fear not fellow hard workers,
Ignore the dream-squashing murmurs…
For they remain blind and dumb to reality,
And will never obtain any unique qualities.

Their narrow minds know not of hardship

Whilst they ride by on their starship.
Keep working harder as they are making you,
One day you'll see, there’s nothing you can’t do.

Beauty beyond my life

As I rise in the morning and feel the sights,
Whether I feel the soft rays of sun on my face,
Or feel the breeze that makes my heart wake,
I know that there is beauty beyond my life.

Struggles I face during the day or night…
Fade as I glance at stars that sparkle and light,
In awe of how much beauty there lies,
I know that there is beauty beyond my life.

To find the words to write and convey,
Whether in a journal, a book, or when I pray,
I stare once again at the endless blue sky,
I know that there is beauty beyond my life.

Success Takes Sacrifice

The more I sacrifice, the better it feels.
At times I doubt how much I can take,
But then I remember everything that's at stake.
Though my mind and body always ache,
The more I sacrifice, the better it feels.

Progression occurs but it's never fast enough,
The audacity; who am I to think I'll pull this off?
A nobody from Slough who can be quite gruff.
But in my heart, I still can't really give up…
Because the more I sacrifice, the better it feels.

I could fail, I could really fucking fail.
Sometimes I miss that miserable, safer trail…
But they say the challenging things are worth it.
And so, the more I sacrifice, the better it feels.

The scariest part is the concept of not failing…
Of finishing that book…
Of starting that business…
Of progressing in this new career…
See, when the sacrifices start to feel so good…
You worry you won't stop when you should.

For that drive, that hunger, is all I know…
What would happen next?

I fear my inner greed will never be full…
And that I may end up finding life rather dull.

Why write?

Women who fought for our rights bravely.
Races that have yet to be given a voice.
Inequalities to be explored and empathised with.
The stigmatised folk from 'other' backgrounds.
Equality; the dream that needs to be spread.

I write because I have something to say…

Whether deemed worthy, I've no control over.
Resolutions need to be made from pen to paper.
India; my ancestors, need acknowledgement.
Therapy; to resolve lifelong inner conflicts.
Empathy; if you felt as I did, you're not alone.

Why do you pick up your pen?
What do you have to say?

Take me back...

To the streets filled with romantic melodies…
To the sights, seeping with history;
Layers and layers of deep history…

Take me back…
To taste more of that flavoursome food filled
with such simple yet incredibly fresh
ingredients…
To the love I can sense in the air,
Poetic paintings and smooth sculptures…

Take me back…
To the moment I realised,
In this perfect place,
That you'd battle to the ends of the earth for me,
That you are the gallantry I subconsciously
sought…
But wait, there is no need; for in my mind now, I
am right back there.

We weren't built in a day; but we were built to
last.
Invicta.

What is my favourite thing about people?

There will be people that scarred you,
There will be people that love you.
There will be people that ignore you,
There will be people that cherish you.
There will be people that laugh at you,
There will be people that encourage you.

But if I were to be asked what my favourite thing is about people,
I believe it's that one inner quality that weaves deep within us like a needle,
When it comes to people, I like to see the good in them,
When a mistake is made, I know we often condemn…
But the best thing about people, is their ability to change,
To evolve, to adapt, like Darwin claimed.

The plan

There was a time when life was truly short,
There was no time to delay or abort,
You'd have to make your life really count,
No time to sit back and have a quick doubt,
But as science and tech advanced, so did life,
People started losing their desire, their drive,
What began as a decade or so of active
adulthood,
Became a longer lifetime of 'could' or 'should',
Moving from when we had no time for planning,
To pre-planning, planning and re-planning,
We lost sight of just being, instead focussed on
'future',
Calculating every single move like a computer,
There was no timeline for a long-term career,
But simply being in the now; the here,
Back then, no one planned away for retirement,
Because frankly, a long life had only been
dreamt,
But as a person's life became longer and longer,
Humankind began to live for planning for the
future,
To the point where life BECAME planning the
future,
They went to school to get into university,

Sticking to a safe path to avoid uncertainty,
Planning to graduate and get a decent job,
Buy a nice house others could be envious of,
Filling the house with lovely, youthful children,
Planning and saving for their children's vision,
Which involved saving for university costs,
So that the kids can get themselves nice jobs,
Then the parents plan how to help them buy a house,
To help them quieten their financial doubts.
The cycle goes on and on and on;
And living for the sake of living has just gone.

Five Rivers

Have you seen anything more quaint?
On top of your home seeing field after field,
Zoning out to take in this beautiful place.
Life's most important priorities, slowly revealed.
Warmly welcomed by a tight-knit community,
Food so rich in culture; spices and salts galore.
This small village, a true picture of ideal unity.
Freshly made food from local farms ensured.
But the big city spreads, trying to take over,
To squash the little peace that remains,
Trying to take over as a money-greedy owner,
Yet communities unite and sustain…
At peace for now, we won the battle,
Attack again, like a tributary, we join and rattle.

www.ingramcontent.com/pod-product-compliance
Lightning Source LLC
Chambersburg PA
CBHW051747130826
49812CB00033B/1043
9789357442459